Understanding the
Bill of
Rights

James Wolfe and Nancy L. Stair

Enslow Publishing

101 W. 23rd Street
Suite 240
New York, NY 10011
USA

enslow.com

Published in 2016 by Enslow Publishing, LLC.
101 W. 23rd Street, Suite 240, New York, NY 10011

Library of Congress Cataloging-in-Publication Data
Wolfe, James, 1960- author.
 Understanding the Bill of Rights / James Wolfe and Nancy L. Stair.
    pages cm. — (Primary sources of American political documents)
 Includes bibliographical references and index.
 Summary: "Discusses the creation and execution of the Bill of Rights in the early days of the United States"—Provided by publisher.
 ISBN 978-0-7660-6882-7
1. United States. Constitution. 1st-10th Amendments—Juvenile literature. 2. Civil rights—United States—Juvenile literature. I. Stair, Nancy L., author. II. Title.
 KF4749.W65 2015
 342.7308'5—dc23

                    2015008044

Printed in the United States of America

To Our Readers: We have done our best to make sure all Web site addresses in this book were active and appropriate when we went to press. However, the author and the publisher have no control over and assume no liability for the material available on those Web sites or on any Web sites they may link to. Any comments or suggestions can be sent by e-mail to customerservice@enslow.com.

Photo Credits: Aaron Haupt/Science Source/Getty Images, p. 79; Allies Interactive/Shutterstock.com (title page, front matter, back matter, and chapter openers); Archive Photos/Getty Images, p. 27; Augusto Cabral/Shutterstock.com (primary source corner dingbat); De Agostini Picture Library/Getty Images, p. 30; DEA/M. SEEMULLER/De Agostini Picture Library/Getty Images, p. 60; DEA Picture Library/De Agostini Picture Library/Getty Images, pp. 14, 50, 68; Everett Historical/Shutterstock.com, pp. 12, 96, 97; Fine Arts Images/Superstock/Getty Images, p. 6; I. Pilon/Shutterstock.com, p. 36; John Parrot/Stocktreck Images/Getty Images, pp. 39, 74, 83; © JT Vintage/age fotostock, p. 88; Library of Congress Prints and Photographs Division, pp. 8, 10, 18, 19, 23, 25, 28, 32, 34, 46, 54, 70; Photri Images/Superstock/Getty Images, pp. 42, 65; Pigprox/Shutterstock.com, p. 58; Superstock/Getty Images, pp. 1, 17, 48; traveler1116/E+/Getty Images, pp. 63, 72.

Cover Credits: Superstock/Getty Images (Patrick Henry Addressing the House of Burgesses); Allies Interactive/Shutterstock.com (title splash); Augusto Cabral/Shutterstock.com (logo and spine button).

Contents

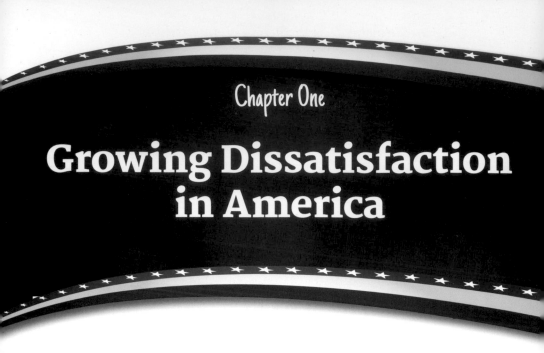

Chapter One

Growing Dissatisfaction in America

Congress shall make no law respecting an establishment of religion, or prohibiting the free exercise thereof; or abridging the freedom of speech, or of the press; or the right of the people peaceably to assemble, and to petition the Government for a redress of grievances.

—Article l, Amendments to the US Constitution

The European colonists who came to the New World did so for different reasons. Some sought religious freedom, while others hoped for better economic opportunities than were available in their homelands. Others were brought as indentured servants or slaves. Their justifications for leaving their mother country had to be strong because living in the new colonies in the seventeenth and eighteenth centuries was extremely difficult. Colonists had to contend with unfamiliar and sometimes harsh climates, strange food, disease, lack of drinkable water, and hostile neighbors.

But the rewards of coming to the New World could also be great. The class system in the Old World, Europe, was very rigid. The class you were born into determined your station in life, your career, and the prospects for your own children. At that point in history, land equaled wealth. The European aristocracy owned most of the land, and most other people worked for them as tenant farmers. In the Americas, people could start fresh, because land was plentiful and there was no aristocracy. The hardships the colonists faced gave them a fierce loyalty to one another, to their colonies, and to the land on which they lived. Far from the king and the harsh class system of England, the settlers felt like free citizens.

Because they were British, the colonists were loyal subjects of the English king, George III. They fought with the British against the French from 1756 to 1763 in the French and Indian War. Known to the English as the Seven Years' War, this conflict started in the colonies and expanded to Europe and

The American colonists sought independence from the tyrannical rule of King George III (1738–1820).

Asia. In 1763, the English won the war and took over large French holdings of land in North America.

But in just thirteen years, between 1763 and 1776, the colonists were transformed from loyal subjects to rebels. There were many reasons. Chief among them were the oppressive acts of the English monarchy and the colonists' desire for freedom. The wealthy elite of the colonies, the men who would eventually write the laws that formed the United States, had had enough of sharing their wealth with the mother country. They were ready to sever all ties with England and keep their money for themselves.

A Series of Prohibitive Acts

The French and Indian War was a great victory for the British, but it doubled the empire's debt. The British Parliament raised taxes throughout the empire, and the American colonies were no exception. In fact, the king felt that since his soldiers were in the colonies to protect the people against foreign and Indian attacks, the colonies should pay more than their fair share of taxes to help support England's defense budget.

From 1763 through 1765, Parliament enacted several laws that angered the American colonists. The Proclamation of 1763 prevented settlement of the area west of the Appalachians, cutting off

England and France fought the Seven Years' War, known commonly as the French and Indian War, over control of North American territory. Britain's success in the war brought with it great debt that negatively impacted the American colonies.

the colonists' supply of new land. This prevented westward expansion. The Currency Act prohibited the use of paper money for the payment of debt. The Sugar Act placed a tax on goods imported into the colonies, such as sugar, wine, and coffee, and was strictly enforced. The Quartering Act required colonists to board soldiers in their own homes upon demand.

These abuses by the British eventually led to the Bill of Rights. The colonists wanted to ensure that they would never again be so exploited and personally violated by their own rulers. Early American mistrust of government power came from the colonial experience itself. Most historians believe that the pivotal event was the Stamp Act, passed by the English Parliament in 1765. This act imposed taxes on all printed documents. The colonists had to purchase authorizing stamps before they could issue newspapers, books, pamphlets, legal documents, and even marriage licenses and playing cards. The Stamp Act so enraged the colonists that they decided they had to fight back against the oppression of the British government.

Even more than the laws themselves, the colonists resented the fact that these taxes were imposed by a distant government in which they were not represented. For years, British soldiers had lived in the midst of the colonies and intimidated the settlers. Furthermore, British soldiers stationed in the colonies could demand to stay in anyone's home. The colonists were further enraged by the way in which the Stamp Act was enforced.

Armed with "writs of assistance" issued by Parliament, British customs inspectors entered people's homes even if they had no evidence of a Stamp Act violation. These soldiers ransacked the people's belongings in search of papers without

Patrick Henry delivered a scathing oratory protesting the Stamp Act in the House of Burgesses in 1765.

stamps—and whatever else they could find. The colonists hated these searches, which became a rallying point for opposition to British rule. These searches eventually led the Founding Fathers to pass the Fourth Amendment of the Bill of Rights, which prevents unreasonable search and seizure.

The Sons of Liberty

From these experiences, the colonists began to see the power of the government and the freedom of the governed as part of a delicate balancing act. When power goes unmonitored or unchecked, it is abused. The nation's founders believed that containing the government's power and protecting the liberty of its citizens were vital. They declared a new purpose for government: the protection of individual rights. Government was to be the instrument of the people's welfare. By itself, the Stamp Act might not have started a revolution, but combined with all the previous acts it compelled the colonists to demand changes.

The colonists strongly denounced the Stamp Act. The wealthy among them were the ones most affected, especially businesspeople, merchants, journalists, lawyers, and other powerful people. These were also the people in positions to demand

> ## ADVERTISEMENT.
>
> THE Members of the Affociation of the Sons of Liberty, are requefted to meet at the City-Hall, at one o'Clock, To-morrow, (being Friday) on Bufi-nefs of the utmoft Importance ;—And every other Friend to the Liberties, and Trade of America, are hereby moft cordially invited, to meet at the fame Time and Place. *The Committee of the Affociation.*
>
> Thurfday, NEW-YORK, 16th December, 1773.

Some colonial leaders came together to form the Sons of Liberty, an organized, underground group that agitated in order to protest Britain's prohibitive laws.

and make changes. Among them were Samuel Adams, Christopher Gadsden, Patrick Henry, John Dickinson, John Lamb, Joseph Warren, and Paul Revere. They formed a group called the Sons of Liberty to organize opposition to the Stamp Act. Merchants boycotted English goods. Colonists drove stamp distributors out of business and destroyed their stamps. But most important, the Massachusetts legislature called for a general congress of the thirteen colonies to figure out how to resist the law. For the first time, the colonies would unite.

The Sons of Liberty was a secret organization formed in the American colonies in the summer of 1765 to oppose the Stamp Act. The group took its name from a speech given in the British Parliament by Isaac Barré in February of 1765, in which he referred to the colonists who had opposed unjust British measures as the "sons of liberty." They supported the boycotts of British goods, forced British stamp distributors to quit their work, and destroyed their stamps.

The Sons of Liberty started agitating against the British government in August 1765, and by the end of that year they had groups in every colony. They shared information. The Sons of Liberty published pamphlets and encouraged the colonists to resist enforcement of the Stamp Act. They sometimes used violent means to force stamp distributors throughout the colonies to resign. The groups also applied pressure to merchants who did not comply with the boycott. The Sons of Liberty drummed up even more support through the newspapers. Many printers and publishers, who would pay the most in duties, were sympathetic to the cause. Nearly every newspaper in the colonies carried daily reports of the activities of the Sons of Liberty. Accounts of their most dramatic escapades spread

One of the Sons of Liberty's most fervent leaders was Samuel Adams (1722–1803). As a delegate in the Continental Congress, Adams called for independence from Britain.

throughout the colonies. These stories inspired citizens and legislatures in every colony to resist the Stamp Act. When the Stamp Act became effective in November 1765, nearly all of these papers went right on publishing without the required stamp.

In early 1766, the Sons of Liberty were causing so much trouble for the British that the royal governors of the colonies were forced to go into hiding. The colonists they relied on to keep the peace were mostly members of the Sons of Liberty. The Sons of Liberty managed to quash the royal government's enforcement of the Stamp Act in nearly every colony.

Declaration of Rights and Grievances

The Stamp Act Congress met in October 1765 in New York City. Delegates came from New York, New Jersey, Rhode Island, Massachusetts, Pennsylvania, Delaware, South Carolina, Maryland, and Connecticut. The congress adopted a Declaration of Rights and Grievances that declared that freeborn Englishmen could not be taxed without their consent. They sent it to King George and the British Parliament. Parliament repealed the Stamp Act in 1766, but not in direct response to the colonists' demands. In fact, it was British merchants and exporters who pressured Parliament to repeal the Stamp Act. The colonists' boycotts had cost British merchants a lot of money!

Probably because it had not fully understood the colonists' fury over the Stamp Act, the English Parliament again levied a direct tax on the colonies in 1767. The Townshend Acts placed duties on many imported items such as glass, paper, paint, and tea. Again, the colonists rebelled against the tax by boycotting these goods. This time, the British sent in more troops to scare the colonists into resuming trade. American politicians, including Benjamin Franklin, called for the repeal of the acts and the return of the troops to England. Parliament was determined to maintain the troops. But, as before, the colonists' boycott hurt British business, and in 1770 Parliament repealed most of the acts.

Boston Massacre and the Tea Party

In 1770, things boiled over in Boston. An unruly mob confronted a small group of British soldiers guarding the Customs House. They threw snowballs at the soldiers, but the soldiers returned fire with bullets, killing five colonists. This infamous incident was called the Boston Massacre. The soldiers were tried and acquitted. They were defended in court by John Adams. More than half of Boston's population

Benjamin Franklin (1706–1790) was a royalist deeply in love with England. His early role in the revolution was one of negotiator between the colonies and England.

PRIMARY SOURCE

The Boston Massacre was one spark that lit the fire of revolution. Already on edge, the colonists resented the presence of British soldiers in Boston.

turned out for the funeral processions. Finally, the British withdrew their extra troops.

In 1773, Parliament passed a Tea Act designed to help the financially strapped East India Company. To finance the East India Company's expensive expansion into India, Parliament eliminated taxes on the company's tea. Further, the act gave the company a monopoly on all tea exported to the colonies, an exemption on export taxes, and a refund of duties on tea it had already paid. Tea shipped to the colonies could be transported only in East India Company ships and sold only through its own agents. The company was able to sell tea at lower prices, giving it an unfair advantage over smaller colonial shippers and merchants and hurting their businesses. Samuel Adams and his Sons of Liberty

THE DESTRUCTION OF TEA AT BOSTON HARBOR.

The Boston Tea Party, believed to have been spearheaded by Samuel Adams, shocked Parliament, who seemed to have no understanding of how its laws had frustrated the colonists.

vowed to fight this outrage, and they were joined by the normally conservative merchants.

The colonists tried to prevent this tea from even arriving in America. They were successful in New York and Philadelphia. At Charleston, the tea landed but was held in warehouses. At Boston, three tea ships arrived and remained unloaded in the harbor. On the night of December 16, 1773, a group of indignant colonists, led by Samuel Adams, Paul Revere, and others, disguised themselves as Native Americans, boarded the ships, and threw the tea into Boston Harbor. The Boston Tea Party was a turning point, bringing the colonists in direct opposition to the British authorities.

Trying desperately to enforce order and authority in Boston, England attempted to force the colonists to pay for the ruined tea. When the colonists refused, British Parliament further limited their freedoms by passing the Coercive Acts. Called the Intolerable Acts by the people of Boston, these laws closed Boston's port and limited citizens' freedom to travel. Furious, the colonists called on the rest of the American colonies to find a solution to England's tightening grip. They began to plan the First Continental Congress.

Chapter Two

Breaking Free From England

The right of the people to be secure in their persons, houses, papers, and effects, against unreasonable searches and seizures, shall not be violated, and no Warrants shall issue, but upon probable cause, supported by Oath or affirmation, and particularly describing the place to be searched, and the persons or things to be seized.

—Article IV, Amendments to the US Constitution

Called by the Sons of Liberty and their supporters, the First Continental Congress convened to protest the Intolerable Acts. It was not the first formal congress to protest England, of course. In 1764, a similar response had been called to protest the Stamp Act. Now, however, frustration was at an all-time high and tensions were thicker. On September 5, 1774, fifty-six delegates from all of the colonies—except Georgia—gathered at Philadelphia's Carpenter's Hall to form the First Continental Congress. This meeting would mark a turning point for the colonies on their road to independence.

The First Continental Congress included many individuals who would later become famous, such as Patrick Henry, George Washington, John Adams and Samuel Adams, John Jay, and John Dickinson. Peyton Randolph of Virginia was unanimously elected as president of the congress. This was the first time the terms "president" and "congress" were used to describe government officials or leaders. Of course, at this point the president had no powers, and his job was merely to preside over the meetings of the delegates and maintain decorum during the debates. Charles Thomson of Pennsylvania was elected secretary and held this office during the fifteen-year life of the Congress.

The Goals of the Congress

To unite the delegates, one vote was granted to each colony regardless of its size. Most of the delegates wanted to discuss the unfair British tax policies, but a few radical members brought up the idea of

As a delegate in the First Continental Congress, John Adams (1735–1826) called for independence from Britain when many others simply wanted reformed tax laws.

declaring independence and breaking away from England altogether. Delegate Joseph Galloway wanted to reconcile with England and reestablish the colonies under a new imperial scheme. He proposed a scheme for self-government to the colonies while maintaining allegiance to the mother country, but the other delegates rejected his ideas. (When the Revolutionary War broke out, Galloway sided with the British and returned to England in 1778.)

The delegates wrote and ratified a declaration of personal rights for the colonists, guaranteeing them the rights to life, liberty, property, assembly, and trial by jury. This document was a precursor to the Bill of Rights. The delegates also drafted a declaration to the king and Parliament, outlining the position of the Congress. This work is called the Declaration of Rights and Grievances. The declaration denounced England's policy of taxation without representation and the presence of the British army in the colonies without the colonists' consent.

In October, the Congress put together several lists of grievances, written principally by John Dickinson. The delegates petitioned the English authorities to correct a number of policies toward the colonies going back to 1763. The First

Pennsylvania delegate John Dickinson (1732–1808) had used his considerable writing talents to sway public opinion against many of Britain's policies.

Continental Congress's most important act was the creation of the Continental Association, which forbade the importation of British goods and the export of all colonial products, except rice, to Britain and the British West Indies. The final act of the first Congress was to set a date for another Congress to meet and consider further steps against the Crown. They agreed to meet again on May 10, 1775. The delegates sent their grievances to the king, and the First Congressional Congress was adjourned.

The Shot Heard 'Round the World

The best way England knew how to subdue rebellion was by sending in troops. The British military was powerful and experienced. Knowing that a confrontation was inevitable, the colonists began to train farmers, peasants, and shopkeepers to be ready to fight on a minute's notice. This is why they were called minutemen.

The colonists did not have to wait long to put their new skills to use. The first shots starting the Revolution were fired at Lexington, Massachusetts, on April 19, 1775. General Thomas Gage commanded the garrison at Boston. Gage's duty in the colonies had been to enforce the Coercive Acts. When news reached him that the Massachusetts colonists were collecting military stores at the town

The first shots of the revolution were heard in Lexington, Massachusetts, when British troops fired on a band of colonial minutemen as they demonstrated peacefully.

of Concord, Gage sent seven hundred soldiers to confiscate these munitions.

The British troops reached the village of Lexington in the early morning and saw a band of seventy minutemen formed in front of them. The minutemen intended only a silent protest. The leader of the minutemen, Captain John Parker, told his troops not to fire unless they were fired at first. The Americans were withdrawing when someone fired a shot, which led the British troops to fire at the minutemen. The British then charged with

This minuteman statue is inscribed with Captain John Parker's orders: "Stand your ground; don't fire unless fired upon, but if they mean to have war, let it begin here."

bayonets, leaving eight dead and ten wounded. It was, in the often quoted phrase of Ralph Waldo Emerson, "the shot heard 'round the world." The countryside was in uproar. As the soldiers marched back to Boston they were continuously fired upon. War had begun.

Smoke from the battles of Lexington and Concord had scarcely cleared when the Second Continental Congress met on May 10, 1775, in Philadelphia. The Second Continental Congress claimed authority over all the colonies and established the American Continental Army. Sam Adams, John Adams, Benjamin Franklin, John Hancock, Patrick Henry, and George Washington were some of the delegates. The Second Continental Congress met throughout the Revolutionary War. It had little money and limited means for obtaining more. Under the threat of the British redcoats, the Continental Congress had to move from place to place. It met in Philadelphia from 1775 to 1776; in Baltimore from 1776 to 1777; in Philadelphia again in 1777; in Lancaster, Pennsylvania, in 1777; in York, Pennsylvania, from 1777 to 1778; and in Philadelphia once more after 1778.

By May 15, 1775, the Congress voted to go to war, inducting the colonial militias into a new

John Hancock (1737–1793) was identified by the British as a dangerous rebel leader. Hancock and Adams fled Boston for Lexington upon hearing that British forces intended to capture them. This prompted Paul Revere's famous midnight ride to Lexington, with warnings of the British approach.

Continental Army and appointing Colonel George Washington of Virginia as commander in chief of the American forces. In the meantime, the Americans would suffer high casualties at Bunker Hill just outside Boston. Congress also ordered American expeditions to march northward into Canada by fall. Although the Americans later captured Montreal, they failed in a winter assault on Quebec and eventually retreated to New York.

King George refused the first Congress's demands. Many in Congress still wanted to try to resolve the issue peacefully, despite the fighting at Concord and Lexington and Bunker Hill. The Congress met throughout the spring and summer, conducting national business such as setting standards for the conduct of trade, establishing currency, and the appointment of foreign diplomats to strike alliances. King George declared the colonies to be rebellious and treasonous and sent 12,000 Hessian (German) mercenaries to North America to suppress the uprising.

There were mixed feelings among the delegates over what to do about the continued hostile acts of the British Parliament. Some delegates wanted immediate independence. Others were still loyal to King George III and, even though they did not like

The Battle of Bunker Hill was significant for the colonies. Though they were defeated, they saw that they could win subsequent battles and perhaps the war.

the British taxes, they wanted to avoid an all-out war with England. The colonies were by no means united in their opposition to the mother country. Approximately half of the colonial population remained loyal to Britain throughout the struggle for independence. If the rebels were to succeed in the coming struggle, some kind of compromise would be necessary.

Despite the outbreak of armed conflict, the idea of complete separation from England was still frightening to some members of the Continental

Congress. In July, John Dickinson drafted a resolution, known as the Olive Branch Petition, begging the king to prevent further hostile actions until some sort of agreement could be worked out. King George III would not read it. He issued a proclamation on August 23, 1775, declaring the colonies to be in a state of rebellion.

The majority of the Congress was not convinced that independence was the right move. It took a fifty-page pamphlet to change their minds. In January 1776, Thomas Paine, a political theorist and writer who had come to America from England in 1774, published *Common Sense*. Within three months 100,000 copies had been sold. Paine attacked the idea of a hereditary monarchy. He presented the alternatives: continued submission to a tyrannical king and an outworn government, or liberty and happiness as a self-sufficient, independent republic. Circulated throughout the colonies, *Common Sense* helped to crystallize the desire for liberty.

The main problem the Continental Congress faced was how to finance the cost of the war. This took a lot of time, and they tried different ways to support their army. Soon the problem of "states' rights" came to the fore, because even though they wanted to be united as one country, each colony

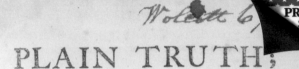

Wolcott 6

PLAIN TRUTH;

ADDRESSED TO THE

INHABITANTS

OF

AMERICA,

Containing, Remarks

ON A LATE PAMPHLET,

entitled

COMMON SENSE:

Wherein are shewn, that the Scheme of INDEPENDENCE is Ruinous, Delusive, and Impracticable: That were the Author's Asseverations, Respecting the Power of AMERICA, as Real as Nugatory; Reconciliation on liberal Principles with GREAT BRITAIN, would be exalted Policy: And that circumstanced as we are, Permanent Liberty, and True Happiness, can only be obtained, by HONORABLE CONNECTIONS, with that Kingdom.

WRITTEN BY CANDIDUS.

Dock Smith of Phila

Will ye turn from flattery, and attend to this Side.?

There TRUTH, unlicenc'd, walks; and dares accost
Even Kings themselves, the Monarchs of the Free!

THOMSON on the Liberties of BRITAIN.

PHILADELPHIA:
Printed, and Sold, by R. BELL, in Third-Street.

MDCCLXXVI.

City of Washington

Thomas Paine's pamphlet *Common Sense* made the case for independence and was responsible for swaying the opinions of the colonists.

wanted to remain independent and make its own laws. The delegates issued paper money and set up a system where the government would borrow money from its citizens and pay it back with interest. They even created a postal system, and the first American navy was formed. There was never any power given to the Congress to levy taxes to finance the war effort. This meant that any support of the army would come from the different colonies or persons who could afford to support them. During the war, General Washington continually pleaded with Congress to authorize funds for his soldiers.

State Constitutions

In May 1776, Congress passed a resolution advising the colonies to form new state governments. These new state constitutions revealed the impact of democratic ideas on the new Americans. The state constitutions ensured the rights that the colonists had fought so hard to gain. Each constitution began with a bill of rights. Virginia's, which served as a model for all the others, included a declaration of principles such as popular sovereignty, rotation in office, and free elections. It also set forth a number of fundamental human liberties: moderate bail and humane punishment, speedy trials by jury, freedom of the press, and the right of the majority to reform or change the government.

Other states enlarged the list of liberties to guarantee the freedom of speech and the freedom of assembly. Many state constitutions included provisions such as the right to bear arms and the right to equal protection under the law. All of the new state constitutions followed the three-branch structure of government, with the executive,

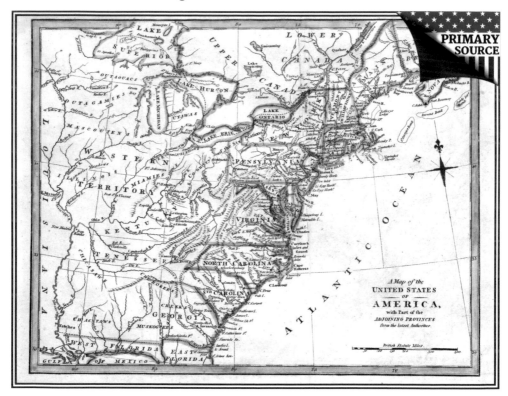

PRIMARY SOURCE

This original map shows the thirteen colonies and the Western Territory. The delegates were aware that the government they were framing would affect new states as well.

legislative, and judicial branches each checked and balanced by the others.

The state constitutions had some limitations, particularly by modern standards. Constitutions written to guarantee people their natural rights failed to secure the most fundamental natural right, that of equality. The colonies south of Pennsylvania excluded their slave populations from their inalienable rights as human beings. Women had no political rights. No state went so far as to permit universal male suffrage, and even in those states that permitted all taxpayers to vote (Delaware, North Carolina, and Georgia, in addition to Pennsylvania), officeholders were required to own a certain amount of property.

Virginia's Precursor to the Bill of Rights

The Virginia Declaration of Rights was written in May 1776 and is considered the basis for the Declaration of Independence, the French Declaration of the Rights of Man, and the Bill of Rights. In the Virginia Declaration of Rights, George Mason called for American independence to preserve Americans' fundamental rights. Virginia's Declaration of Rights provided much of the inspiration for the Bill of Rights. Thomas Jefferson also drew upon it for the opening paragraphs of the

Declaration of Independence. It was adopted by the Virginia Constitutional Convention on June 12, 1776.

The Declaration of Rights was drafted by George Mason, with a small but significant modification by James Madison. Mason called for government tolerance of the exercise of religion, while Madison argued that the free exercise of religion was not simply to be tolerated by the authorities, but was a right. Historians think Thomas Jefferson received a copy of the Virginia Declaration of Rights directly from Mason and Richard Henry Lee, his fellow Virginia planters and revolutionaries. Jefferson drew extensively from the Virginia Declaration of Rights, as well as from his own drafts of a new constitution for Virginia, as he was composing the Declaration of Independence in June 1776.

For example, the Virginia Declaration of Rights proposes "that all men are born equally free and independent, and have certain inherent natural Rights . . . among which are the Enjoyment of Life and Liberty, with the Means of acquiring and possessing property, and pursuing and obtaining Happiness and Safety." The Declaration of Independence states "that all men are created equal, that they are endowed by their creator with certain

Virginia delegate Thomas Jefferson (1743–1826) drew upon the Virginia Declaration of Rights, among other writings, when John Adams selected him to draft the Declaration of Independence in 1776.

inalienable rights, that among these are life, liberty, and the pursuit of happiness."

Mason's draft, which included several clauses added by Lee, was used by James Madison in preparing the Bill of Rights, and by the Marquis de Lafayette in drafting the French Declaration of the Rights of Man.

On May 10, 1776—one year to the day since the Second Continental Congress had first met—a resolution was adopted calling for separation from England. Now only a formal declaration was needed. In June 7, 1776, Virginia delegate Richard Henry Lee proposed that the colonies unite and declare themselves independent of Britain. A committee was formed to look into the question of independence. It was made up of John Adams, Ben Franklin, Robert Livingston, Roger Sherman, and Thomas Jefferson. Jefferson was well regarded as a writer and was also needed to balance the northern delegates on the committee. He presented the draft of the Declaration of Independence to the committee within a few days. The committee forwarded it on to the Congress after some revisions.

A Formal Declaration

The Declaration of Independence was formally ratified by the Continental Congress on July 4, 1776.

Originally written by Jefferson, the document as we know it today is not entirely his, as the independence committee made a number of revisions to his draft. Jefferson forwarded a marked-up copy of his first draft to Franklin, asking for his advice. Once the committee was satisfied with the Declaration it was sent to the full Congress for approval.

For two days, July 2 and 3, the Congress worked on the declaration. It was a harsh attack on the king. Jefferson's first two paragraphs, with their strong and patriotic wording, were left mostly untouched. But Jefferson was much too wordy in his listing of the crimes of the king. The Declaration of Independence is divided into three sections: a preamble, a list of grievances or justifications, and finally the declaration of separation. Much of the preamble came from George Mason's previous work, the Virginia Declaration of Rights. Published just days after Richard Henry Lee's proposition to the Congress, Jefferson borrowed heavily from the work.

The preamble establishes that all men have rights, that the government is established to secure those rights, and if and when a government tries to take away those rights it should be abolished. Listed next are almost thirty separate points detailing the

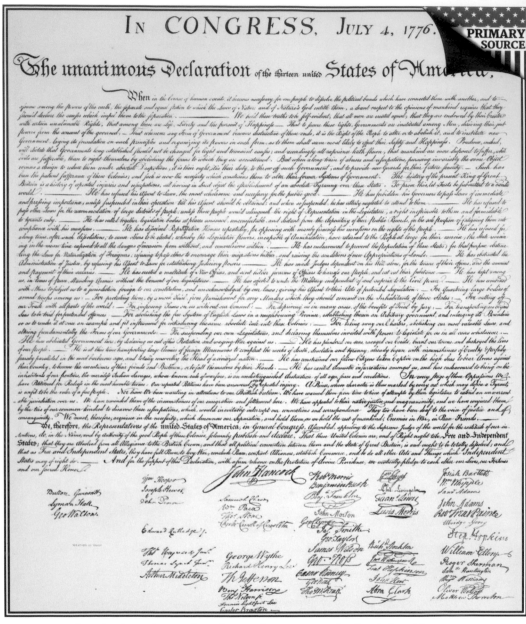

The Declaration of Independence was drafted by Thomas Jefferson and revised by the other members of the Committee of Five appointed by Congress. The declaration has since been an inspiration for other countries declaring independence.

crimes of the king against the people of the colonies. It vows that the new nation has no lasting grudge against the people of Britain, but that it would fight them if necessary. Finally, the conclusion of the document declares that "the good People of these Colonies, solemnly publish and declare, That these United Colonies are, and of Right ought to be Free and Independent States."

The Declaration of Independence was ratified on July 4, 1776, two days after Congress voted to accept it. On July 8, the declaration was proclaimed at a crowded public gathering at Philadelphia's state house. On August 2, 1776, the document was signed, printed out, and distributed on horseback to the colonies. As the news spread, American colonists cheered, celebrated, and removed symbols of Britain. Effigies of the king were burned in town squares. A new, fiercely independent nation was born.

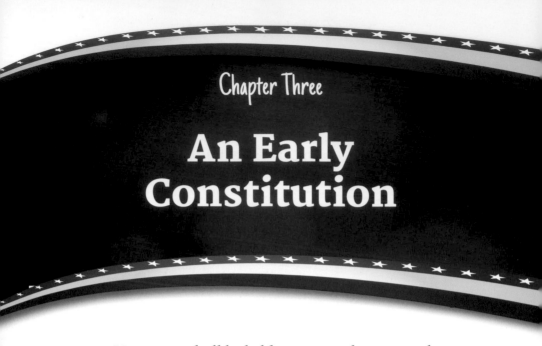

Chapter Three

An Early Constitution

No person shall be held to answer for a capital, or otherwise infamous crime, unless on a presentment or indictment of a Grand Jury, except in cases arising in the land or naval forces, or in the Militia, when in actual service in time of War or public danger; nor shall any person be subject for the same offence to be twice put in jeopardy of life or limb; nor shall be compelled in any criminal case to be a witness against himself, nor be deprived of life, liberty, or property, without due process of law; nor shall private property be taken for public use, without just compensation.

—Article V, Amendments to the US Constitution

Once independence was officially declared, the colonies needed to set about formally setting up their new government. There were a number of decisions that would need to be made. For example, while it was important to acknowledge individual states' rights, they realized that they would need a united front to stand up to powerhouse nations like England. None of the states would have been able to fund the Revolutionary War alone.

The Articles of Confederation

Thus, the delegates of the Second Constitutional Convention set about framing a national constitution. The document they created, the Articles of Confederation, became the basis for the US government and a precursor to the US Constitution. Because the Articles were not entirely successful, they were replaced with the Constitution of the United States. But they did serve the new nation for a decade. The Articles of Confederation were America's first attempt to govern itself as an independent nation, and the first attempt at establishing a national government in the New World. The Articles formally renamed the colonies as states and united them as a confederation, or a loose league of states represented in a Congress.

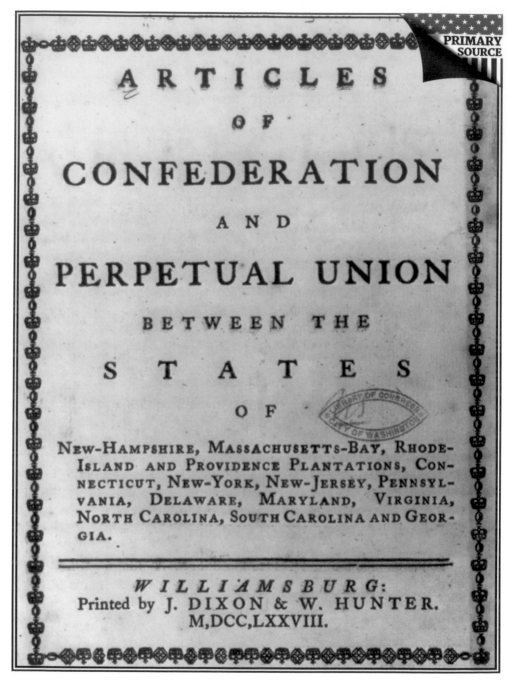

ARTICLES

OF

CONFEDERATION

AND

PERPETUAL UNION

BETWEEN THE

S T A T E S

OF

NEW-HAMPSHIRE, MASSACHUSETTS-BAY, RHODE-ISLAND AND PROVIDENCE PLANTATIONS, CONNECTICUT, NEW-YORK, NEW-JERSEY, PENNSYLVANIA, DELAWARE, MARYLAND, VIRGINIA, NORTH CAROLINA, SOUTH CAROLINA AND GEORGIA.

WILLIAMSBURG:
Printed by J. DIXON & W. HUNTER.
M,DCC,LXXVIII.

The Articles of Confederation served as America's first constitution. They were replaced in 1789.

The Articles of Confederation were first proposed by a committee headed by John Dickinson on July 12, 1776. Because of the war and disagreements between the colonies, it took three and a half years to get final ratification of the Articles, which had to be ratified by each and every state. All of the states finally ratified the Articles on March 1, 1781. The war officially ended two years later in April 1783.

The Third Continental Congress, which got underway on December 20, 1776, modified and finalized the Articles of Confederation. On November 15, 1777, the Articles were proposed to the colonies. The Articles originally proposed by Dickinson and his committee were greatly changed before being passed on to the colonies. Originally, for example, the Articles called for a strong central government, a feature the ratified Articles lacked. Meanwhile, Americans suffered severe setbacks on the battlefields for months after independence was declared. But their hard work and perseverance would eventually pay off.

France began providing aid to the colonies in May 1776, when it sent fourteen ships with war supplies to America. In fact, most of the gunpowder used by the American armies came from France. France saw an opportunity to weaken its ancient

Congress adopted the final draft of the Articles of Confederation on November 15, 1777. However, the articles still needed to be ratified by all thirteen states. Maryland held out until 1781.

enemy, Britain, and restore the power it had lost in the Seven Years' War (the French and Indian War). On February 6, 1778, America and France signed a Treaty of Amity and Commerce, in which France recognized America as a nation. They also signed a Treaty of Alliance, which stipulated that if France entered the war neither country would quit fighting until America won its independence.

The French-American alliance broadened the Revolution into a world war. In June 1778, British ships fired on French vessels. In 1779, Spain, hoping to reacquire territories taken by Britain in the Seven Years' War, entered the conflict on the side of France, but not as an ally of the Americans. In 1780, Britain declared war on the Dutch, who had continued to trade with the Americans. The combination of these European powers, with France in the lead, was a far greater threat to Britain than the American colonies standing alone.

The British government decided to pursue peace negotiations in Paris in early 1782, with the American side represented by Benjamin Franklin, John Adams, and John Jay. In February 1783, King George III issued his Proclamation of Cessation of Hostilities. On April 15, 1783, Congress approved the final treaty, and Great Britain and its former colonies signed it on September 3. Known as the Treaty of Paris, the peace settlement acknowledged the independence, freedom, and sovereignty of the thirteen colonies. Great Britain gave the new United States the territory west to the Mississippi River, north to Canada, and south to Florida, which was returned to Spain. The colonies became free and independent states.

In addition to giving formal recognition to the United States, the treaty established the boundaries

John Jay (1745–1829) was instrumental in negotiating the Treaty of Paris with the British. This ended the war and officially recognized the United States as an independent nation.

of the country, specified fishing rights, allowed creditors of each country to be paid by citizens of the other, restored the rights and property of Loyalists, opened up the Mississippi River to commerce, and provided for the evacuation of all British forces.

Weaknesses of the Articles of Confederation

Created during the Revolutionary War, the Articles of Confederation reflected the colonists' fears of a strong central government. They were afraid that their individual needs would be ignored by a national government with too much power. Having lived under the harsh rule of the British monarchy, the colonists were well aware of the abuses that often resulted from such power. The delegates wrote the Articles to give the largest share of power to the individual states. Under the Articles, each of the states retained their sovereignty, freedom, and independence.

The Articles created a confederation called the United States of America. In a confederation, the individual political units—in this case states— maintain their sovereignty. In other words, each political unit is self-governing. However, they are joined together in a coordinated way to deal with certain issues, such as security and defense. The independence of each political unit is seen as both the main advantage and main disadvantage of a confederation. To put it into perspective, many confederations have been tried throughout world history, but none survive today.

The Articles had several things wrong with them. They required that all changes be approved unanimously. Several attempts to change the Articles prior to the adoption of the Constitution were held up by one state's refusal to ratify. The Articles gave the United States no power to tax the individual states to maintain the national treasury. The federal government had to rely on the states to pay bills sent to them. However, the bills were often ignored, and since the national government had no power of enforcement, there was little that could be done. In addition, the new nation was unable to repel British and Spanish advances on America's borders because the states would not pay taxes to finance a military force. Furthermore, the United States had no power to regulate commerce between the states, leading to bitter tariff wars between them.

After the war, economic difficulties threatened the new nation. Merchants who had supplied both armies with food, weapons, and other goods now suffered a loss of business. The states gave preference to American goods in their tariff policies, but these tariffs were inconsistent. Farmers suffered the most from economic difficulties following the Revolutionary War as the supply of farm produce exceeded demand. Prices fell. Many farmers fell into debt, and they wanted strong remedies to avoid foreclosure on their properties and imprisonment for debt. Courts were clogged with suits for debt.

All through the summer of 1786, popular conventions and informal gatherings in several states demanded reform in the state administrations. In January 1786, the government of Virginia called for a meeting of the states at Annapolis to talk about modifying the Articles of Confederation. Only five states sent delegates to the meeting at Annapolis. Disappointed, those who did assemble called for another meeting the following May. In the meantime, a popular uprising had begun in Massachusetts, led by a bankrupt farmer named Daniel Shays.

Economic Unrest and Rebellion

In the fall of 1786, mobs of farmers in Massachusetts under Daniel Shays's leadership began to forcibly prevent the county courts from sitting and passing further judgments for farm debt. For six months, Shays and his rebels terrorized the Massachusetts for either.   JAMES

PENNSYLVANIA, ſſ.

By the *Prefident* and the *Supr*
ecutive Council of the Common-
wealth of *Pennſylvania,*

A PROCLAMATION.

WHEREAS the General Aſſembly of this Common-
wealth, by a law entituled 'An act for co-operating with
" the ſtate of Maſſachuſetts bay, agreeable to the articles of
" confederation, in the apprehending of the proclaimed rebels
" DANIEL SHAYS, LUKE DAY, ADAM WHEELER
" and ELI PARSONS," have enacted, " that rewards ad-
" ditional to thoſe offered and promiſed to be paid by the ſtate
" of Maſſachuſetts Bay, for the apprehending the aforeſaid
" rebels, be offered by this ſtate ;"   WE do hereby offer the
following rewards to any perſon or perſons who ſhall, within
the limits of this ſtate, apprehend the rebels aforeſaid, and
ecure them in the gaol of the city and county of Philadelphia,
——— viz. For the apprehending of the ſaid Daniel Shays, and
ſecuring him as aforeſaid, the reward of *One bundred and Fifty
Pounds* lawful money of the ſtate of Maſſachuſetts Bay, and
One Hundred Pounds lawful money of this ſtate ; and for the
apprehending the ſaid Luke Day, Adam Wheeler and Eli
Parſons, and ſecuring them as aforeſaid, the reward (reſpec-
tively) of *One Hundred Pounds* lawful money of Maſſachuſetts
Bay and *Fifty Pounds* lawful money of this ſtate : And all
judges, juſtices, ſheriffs and conſtables are hereby ſtrictly en-
joined and required to make diligent ſearch and enquiry after,
and to uſe their utmoſt endeavours to apprehend and ſecure the
ſaid Daniel Shays, Luke Day, Adam Wheeler and Eli Parſons, their aiders, abettors and comforters, and every of them,
ſo that they may be dealt with according to law.
  GIVEN in Council, under the hand of the Preſident, and
    the Seal of the State, at Philadelphia, this tenth
    day of March, in the year of our Lord one thouſand
    ſeven hundred and eighty-ſeven.
                        BENJAMIN FRANKLIN.
ATTEST
    JOHN ARMSTRONG, jun. Secretary.

This proclamation by the State of Pennsylvania offering a
reward for Daniel Shays and his fellow ringleaders is signed by
Benjamin Franklin.

countryside. The United States found that the Articles of Confederation gave it little power to fight the uprising.

In January 1787, a ragtag army of 1,200 farmers moved toward the federal arsenal in Springfield, Massachusetts. The rebels, armed with staves and pitchforks, were repulsed by a small state militia force. The government captured fourteen rebels and sentenced them to death, but ultimately pardoned some and let the others off with short prison terms. After the defeat of the rebellion, a newly elected legislature, whose majority sympathized with the rebels, met some of their demands for debt relief.

Although Shays's Rebellion had been quashed, there was no telling how many more such acts would spring up in response to economic difficulty. It was becoming increasingly clear that the solution to such unrest was a stronger, more unified government. A delicate balance would need to be achieved.

Chapter Four

Framing the US Constitution

In all criminal prosecutions, the accused shall enjoy the right to a speedy and public trial, by an impartial jury of the State and district wherein the crime shall have been committed, which district shall have been previously ascertained by law, and to be informed of the nature and cause of the accusation; to be confronted with the witnesses against him; to have compulsory process for obtaining witnesses in his favor, and to have the Assistance of Counsel for his defence.

—Article VI, Amendments to the US Constitution

As the rush of achieving independence faded and the reality of new nationhood set, the states began to understand that they would need to formally unify much more than they perhaps had originally intended. The postwar economic recession and other problems between the states were making it perfectly clear that the Articles of Confederation, though carefully drafted and sufficient for a period, were falling short. The Articles would need to be amended.

The Constitutional Convention

The conference of representatives of five states at Annapolis, Maryland, in 1786 was a failure. One of the few delegates who attended, Alexander Hamilton, convinced his colleagues that the situation was too serious and complicated to be dealt with by them alone. He suggested calling all the states to appoint representatives for a meeting to be held the following spring in Philadelphia. The Continental Congress was at first indignant over this bold step, but its protests were cut short by the news that Virginia had elected George Washington to be a delegate. During the next fall and winter, elections were held in all states but Rhode Island, and the delegates prepared to meet.

In May 1787, fifty-five delegates met at the Philadelphia State House. The state legislatures sent leaders with experience in colonial and state governments. GeorgeWashington, regarded as the country's first citizen for his military leadership

The Declaration of Independence and the US Constitution were debated and adopted in the Philadelphia State House.

during the Revolutionary War, was chosen as presiding officer. Prominent among the more active members were two Pennsylvanians: Gouverneur Morris, who saw the need for a strong national government, and James Wilson. Also sent by Pennsylvania was Benjamin Franklin, who was nearing the end of his extraordinary career of public service. From Virginia came James Madison, a practical young statesman and scholar of politics and history. Today he is recognized as the "Father" of the Constitution. Massachusetts sent Rufus King and Elbridge Gerry. Roger Sherman, a shoemaker turned judge, was one of the representatives from Connecticut. From New York came Alexander Hamilton, who had originally proposed the meeting. Absent from the convention were Thomas Jefferson, who was serving in France as minister, and John Adams, serving in the same capacity in Great Britain. The average age of the delegates was forty-two.

Although the convention originally met merely to draft amendments to the Articles of Confederation, led by its more radical members the delegates set aside the Articles and basically built an entirely new form of government. They decided to split the government into three equally powerful

Virginian James Madison (1751–1836) is called the Father of the Constitution because his Virginia Plan broadened the constitutional debates.

branches. Legislative, executive, and judicial powers were to be balanced so that no one branch of the government could ever gain complete control. People feared that a strong central government with vast powers would lead to tyranny. This principle of the separation of powers among the executive, legislative, and judicial branches created a system of checks to maintain the balance between the power and authority of the federal government and the rights and liberties of individual citizens.

The delegates recognized the need to reconcile two different powers: the power of local control, which was already being exercised by the thirteen individual states, and the power of the central government. They adopted the principle that the power of the national government had to be carefully defined, while all other functions and powers would belong to the states. But the central government had to have real power, so the delegates gave the government the authority to coin money, regulate commerce, declare war, and make peace, among other things.

Representatives of the small states objected to changes that would reduce their influence in the national government by basing representation upon population rather than upon statehood, as was the case under the Articles of Confederation. On the other hand, representatives of large states, such as Virginia, wanted their number of representatives based on the state's population. This debate threatened to go on indefinitely until Roger Sherman introduced the idea of representation in proportion to the population of the states in one house of Congress, the House of Representatives, and equal representation in the other, the Senate.

This issue was resolved, but almost every question raised new problems to be addressed only by new compromises. Northerners wanted slaves counted when determining each state's tax share, but not in determining the number of seats a state would have in the House of Representatives. The House of Representatives would be apportioned according to the number of free inhabitants plus three-fifths of the slaves. The three-fifths compromise increased the number of representatives the southern states could have and increased their tax obligations, but failed to grant any political rights to the slaves themselves.

The convention finally put on paper the formal organization of the new government. The delegates gave the federal government full power to levy taxes, borrow money, print currency, grant patents

Roger Sherman signed the Declaration of Independence and helped draft the Articles of Confederation, but his greatest contributions were at the Constitutional Convention.

and copyrights, set up post offices, and build roads. The national government also had the power to raise and maintain an army and navy, and to regulate trade and commerce between the states. It was given the management of Indian affairs, foreign policy, and the power to wage war. It could pass laws for naturalizing foreigners and controlling public lands, and it could admit new states that would have the same powers as the original states.

The US Constitution

The Constitution of the United States has become one of the world's landmark documents and is the oldest written national constitution currently in use in the entire world. It defines the fundamental structure and laws of the United States federal government. On September 28, 1787, the Constitution was submitted to the thirteen states for ratification. By June 1788, nine states had ratified the document. March 4, 1789, was set as the day the new Constitution would take effect.

The Constitution represents a set of general principles out of which state and federal laws, statutes, and codes have emerged. The Constitution has remained the foundation of American government because succeeding Congresses and Supreme Courts have been able to interpret it or

The work of many great and disparate minds, the Constitution of the United States reflects the importance of compromise and careful forethought.

adapt it to the demands of changing times. After it was ratified, Congress began enhancing the definition of constitutional powers through statutes, such as providing for the creation of the federal budget system, executive departments, federal courts, new states and territories, and controlling presidential succession. Many familiar institutions have been recognized by the courts as valid parts of the constitutional system of government. These include political parties, procedures for nominating presidential candidates, the electoral college system, and the appointment of a presidential cabinet.

The first seven articles of the Constitution lay out the organization of the federal government. Article I gives all lawmaking powers to the House of Representatives and the Senate. These legislative bodies have the right to raise taxes, borrow money, regulate interstate commerce, put together military forces, and declare war. Each legislative body was given power to determine its own rules of procedure.

Article II gives executive power to the president, including duties as the chief executive officer and commander in chief of the armed forces, and treaty-making power with the approval of two-thirds of the Senate. The president also has the power to make appointments within the federal government upon approval of the majority of the Senate.

Article III gives the courts judicial power. The Supreme Court of the United States is mandated as the final court of appeal from the lower state and federal courts. The courts interpret the Constitution, which is called the "power of judicial review."

Article IV of the Constitution deals with relations among the states and the rights of citizens of the states. Article V lays down the procedures to amend the Constitution. Article VI deals with public debt. Article VII lays down how to ratify amendments to the Constitution.

Article X states that the federal government has only those powers that are delegated to it explicitly in the Constitution. All other government powers fall to the states. These are called "residual powers," and they state that nothing prescribed by state law can nullify any of the powers granted in the Constitution. Despite the fact that residual powers remained with the states, Congress has the authority to make laws.

After sixteen weeks of deliberation, on September 17, 1787, the finished Constitution was signed by thirty-nine of the forty-two delegates present.

This painting depicts George Washington signing the Constitution at the 1787 Convention of Philadelphia. The delegates realized they still had more work to do.

Rights of the People

After the delegates to the Constitutional Convention had finished the final draft of the Constitution, George Mason noted that the new document contained no declaration of the rights of the people. A number of prominent Americans were alarmed at the omission of individual liberties from the proposed Constitution. Elbridge Gerry of Massachusetts seconded Mason's motion to convene a committee to draft a declaration of rights. But no state voted to convene the committee, and, in protest, Gerry and Mason refused to sign the Constitution. Mason, along with James Madison, had a heavy hand in the writing of the Virginia

Declaration of Rights, which became a model for the Bill of Rights.

Even as the new nation set about to establish a government, people couldn't forget the many civil rights violations committed against them by the British. However, the draft of the Constitution submitted to the states for ratification neglected to address basic human rights. Thomas Jefferson, the minister to France at the time, wrote James Madison that he was concerned about the lack of provisions providing for freedom of religion, freedom of the press, protection against standing armies, and restriction against monopolies. Aware of the lack of these provisions, George Washington urged Congress in his first inaugural address to propose amendments that offered protection to its citizens.

The convention was over and the members had disbanded. But a crucial part of the struggle for a more perfect union was yet to be faced. The consent of popularly elected state conventions was still required before the document could become effective. The delegates had decided that the Constitution would take effect upon ratification of nine of the thirteen states. By June 1788, the required nine states had ratified the Constitution, but the large states of Virginia and New York had not. Most people felt that without the support of these two states the Constitution would not be honored. To many, the document seemed full of dangers. What would stop the strong central government that it established from tyrannizing them, oppressing them with heavy taxes and dragging them into wars?

Elected unanimously, George Washington was inaugurated as the new nation's first president on April 30, 1789. Washington would be reelected to another term in 1792.

Central Government vs. States' Rights

Differing views on these questions led to passionate disagreements among two parties: the Federalists, who favored a strong central government, and the Antifederalists, who preferred a loose association of separate states. The conflict between the Federalists and the Antifederalists had a great impact on American history. The Federalists, led by Alexander Hamilton, represented urban interests, while the Antifederalists, led by Thomas Jefferson, spoke for the rural and southern interests. The debate between the two concerned the power of the central government versus that of the states, with the Federalists favoring the former and the Antifederalists advocating states' rights.

In Virginia, the Antifederalists, led by Patrick Henry, attacked the proposed new government by challenging the opening phrase of the Constitution: "We the People of the United States." Without using the individual state names in the Constitution, the delegates argued, the states would not retain their separate rights or powers. Hamilton sought a strong central government that would support commerce and industry. Jefferson advocated for a decentralized republic. He knew the value of a strong central government in dealing with foreign powers, but he

Patrick Henry was one delegate who disapproved of the Constitution's lack of protection of individual rights and liberties.

did not want it strong enough to suppress the will of the citizens. Hamilton feared anarchy and wanted order. Jefferson feared tyranny and desired freedom.

Alexander Hamilton, John Jay, and James Madison pushed for the ratification of the Constitution in a series of essays known as the *Federalist Papers*. The essays, published in New York newspapers, argued in favor of a central federal government, with separate executive, legislative, and judicial branches that checked and balanced one another. The *Federalist Papers* influenced the New York delegates, and they ratified the Constitution on July 26.

Fear of a strong central government was not the only concern among those who opposed the Constitution. People were also concerned that the Constitution did not adequately protect individual rights and freedoms. Virginian George Mason was one of three delegates to the Constitutional Convention who refused to sign the final document because it did not ensure individual rights. Together with Patrick Henry, he campaigned against ratification of the Constitution by Virginia. Five states, including Massachusetts, ratified the Constitution on the condition that amendments supporting human rights be added immediately.

Alexander Hamilton (1755 or 1757–1804) advocated for a strong central government. His *Federalist Papers* was a series of essays persuading New Yorkers to ratify the Constitution.

The demand for amendments to the Constitution that would protect individual rights were the first order of business when the first Congress met in New York City in September 1789. Congress first adopted twelve amendments, which were considered and debated over many months. Finally, by the end of 1791, ten of the amendments were ratified by enough states to include them in the US Constitution. These ten amendments to the Constitution address the rights of Americans. They are known as the Bill of Rights.

Chapter Five

The First Ten Amendments

In Suits at common law, where the value in controversy shall exceed twenty dollars, the right of trial by jury shall be preserved, and no fact tried by a jury, shall be otherwise re-examined in any Court of the United States, than according to the rules of the common law.

—Article VII, Amendments
to the US Constitution

The Bill of Rights is the name given to the first ten amendments to the US Constitution. The proposed amendments were used as a bargaining chip to achieve ratification of the Constitution. Because Antifederalists were nervous that they were signing over absolute power to a central government, the Federalists agreed to some changes in order to achieve constitutional ratification.

These amendments would ensure personal rights to individuals and limit the US government's power in certain regards.

The most significant guarantees for individual civil rights are provided by the Bill of Rights. The First Amendment guarantees freedom of religion, speech, and the press, as well as the rights of peaceful assembly and petition. Other amendments guarantee the right to own private property, fair treatment of those accused of crimes (such as a prohibition against unreasonable search and seizure), freedom from self-incrimination, a speedy and impartial jury trial, and representation by counsel.

Since the adoption of the Bill of Rights, only seventeen more amendments to the Constitution have been ratified. Although a number of the subsequent amendments revised the federal government's structure and operations, most followed the precedent established by the Bill of Rights and expanded individual rights and freedoms. The first ten amendments were passed together, and the amendments had their own preamble, or introduction:

CONGRESS of the UNITED STATES begun and held at the City of New York, on

Wednesday the Fourth of March, one thousand seven hundred and eighty nine.

The Conventions of a number of the States having at the time of their adopting the Constitution, expressed a desire, in order to prevent misconstruction or abuse of its powers, that further declaratory and restrictive clauses should be added: And as extending the ground of public confidence in the Government, will best insure the beneficent ends of its institution.

RESOLVED by the Senate and House of Representatives of the United States of America, in Congress assembled, two thirds of both Houses concurring, that the following Articles be proposed to the Legislatures of the several States, as Amendments to the Constitution of the United States, all or any of which Articles, when ratified by three fourths of the said Legislatures, to be valid to all intents and purposes, as part of the said Constitution.

Amendment I: Free Speech

The First Amendment to the Constitution states that "Congress shall make no law respecting an establishment of religion, or prohibiting the free exercise thereof; or abridging the freedom of speech, or of the press; or the right of the people peaceably

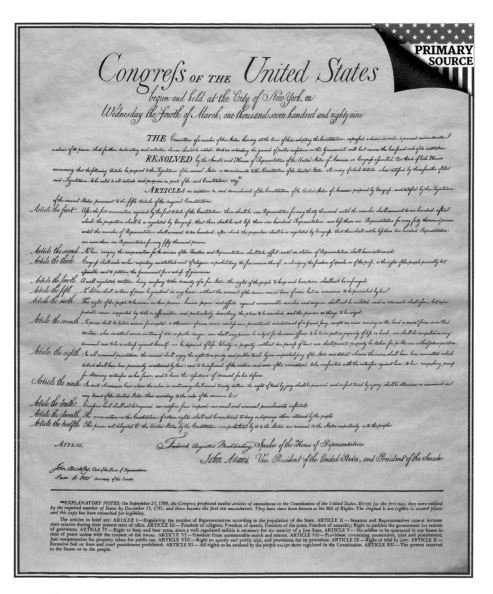

The ten ratified amendments to the Constitution became the Bill of Rights in 1791. These amendments were drafted because the US Constitution did not define or guarantee protection of rights and liberties for individual citizens. Those delegates who opposed the Constitution had worried that the government could descend into tyranny, without such protections for the people.

to assemble, and to petition the Government for a redress of grievances."

The First Amendment gives American citizens the right to think whatever they choose to think. It guarantees freedom of religion, speech, and the press. It covers the right to demonstrate, pass out leaflets, and state opinions in public. It gives American citizens the right to speak or publish their beliefs, no matter how controversial or offensive they might be. People can express whatever they feel like expressing, as long as they behave themselves while doing so. People can even complain about how the government is run without fear of reprisal.

But freedom of speech does not give citizens an unrestricted right to say anything they want. The courts have interpreted the meaning of the amendment in a way that gives governments the right to restrict access to certain kinds of pornography, and to protect the public from lewd or indecent behavior or from speech that is threatening or disrupts public order.

The First Amendment was written because the colonists had been unable to complain freely about the way the British government treated them. Freedom of the press was specifically mentioned because the Founding Fathers believed that, if all else failed, the press should be able to investigate the government and inform the people. The press is often called the "fourth estate," because the founders believed strongly that a free press is just as important as the other three branches of government. The First Amendment has also been interpreted in the courts to include freedom of association and assembly. Free speech applies to ideas you disagree with as well as ideas you agree with. A true believer in free speech will defend the right of everyone to speak freely. The First Amendment also prohibits the government from supporting or endorsing a religion, so as not to give the appearance of favoring one religious view or practice.

Amendment II: A Well-Regulated Militia

The Second Amendment states that "A well regulated Militia, being necessary to the security of a free State, the right of the people to keep and bear Arms, shall not be infringed." The Second Amendment enables each state and the federal government to establish armies for defense comprised of armed citizens. There has been a great deal of debate about this amendment and just what it means over the years. Some people think that this amendment permits Americans the unrestricted right to own their own weapons for personal defense. Some argue that the ultimate protection against the tyranny of our own government is the right of ordinary citizens to use armed force to oppose it. Others believe that the Founding Fathers simply intended that citizens be prepared to be called by their states or the national government to defend the nation as part of regular military units.

Interpretation is further complicated by the fact that we live in a very different country from the one inhabited by men like Jefferson and Madison. Theirs was a nation of farmers, who, if they could afford them, owned firearms to hunt and to defend their frontier farms against attacks by Native Americans. A musket in the home was as valuable as an axe or a plow. After the departure of British troops there was no real standing army in the United States, and it was taken for granted, as the war for independence had shown, that in a time of emergency an army would be formed from those armed citizen-farmers. Today, however, with the national government possessing combined armed services of about three million men and women, well-trained local police forces in almost every community, and no hostile forces on our frontiers, just what is the meaning of the "right of the people to keep and bear Arms"?

The Second Amendment establishes the right of a regulated militia and the right to bear arms. This amendment is often cited by gun rights advocates during debates about gun control, with some controversy.

More than two-hundred years removed from the violence of the Revolutionary War, with our basic liberties taken for granted, many Americans today seek an orderly way of life and are disturbed by the idea of widespread access to firearms. But many others believe that the possession of such weapons is a right guaranteed by the Constitution. Like many of our rules and laws, the application of this right is undergoing constant reinterpretation by the courts and the other branches of government. This debate arises every time there is a high-profile mass murder, like the tragic Columbine High School Massacre in 1999 and the Sandy Hook Elementary School Shooting in 2012.

Amendment III: The Quartering of Soldiers

The Third Amendment states that "No Soldier shall, in time of peace be quartered in any house, without the consent of the Owner, nor in time of war, but in a manner to be prescribed by law." This means specifically that citizens don't have to let soldiers stay in their homes, unless there is a war, and even then only in a manner prescribed by legal authority. The Third Amendment was written after bitter experience with the British during the Revolutionary War, who, both to save the Crown money and to demoralize their colonial subjects, quartered soldiers in private homes. The British therefore had their representatives firmly entrenched within the day-to-day lives of the colonists, making it difficult for citizens to organize any kind of rebellion or even to express themselves freely in their own homes. It is a measure of how much the Founding Fathers feared the potential tyranny of their own central government that such an amendment became part of the fundamental law of the nation even when there was no foreign army to worry about.

Underlying the specific concern about quartering troops in private homes, however, was a deeper principle. It is the idea that the nation's armed forces should be used only to defend the nation from foreign attack, and that these forces should not interfere in the daily lives of the citizens nor enforce criminal or civil law, nor should such forces be used in any way by the government against the people. Shortly after the Civil War this principle was made explicit by passage of the Posse Comitatus Act, which prohibited the army from enforcing civil law. In recent times this has produced some legal conflicts when certain members of the armed services have been called upon to assist regular civilian law-enforcement authorities, as with drug interdiction and antiterrorism efforts. But in general the military provides technical assistance to law enforcement authorities and does not get involved in searches, seizures, and arrests.

Amendment IV: Unreasonable Search and Seizure

The Fourth Amendment states that "The right of the people to be secure in their persons, houses, papers, and effects, against unreasonable searches and seizures, shall not be violated, and no Warrants shall issue, but upon probable cause, supported by Oath or affirmation, and particularly describing the place to be searched, and the persons or things to be seized."

This means that citizens can refuse to have themselves, their homes, their personal records, and their possessions searched or taken away, unless a warrant is issued by a judge. A warrant can only be issued if a law enforcement officer can convince a judge that there is a reasonable cause for suspicion that a person has committed a crime. Law enforcement officials and representatives of the government cannot make this determination on their own. An independent jurist must evaluate the government's claim that a citizen is a danger to the community. A warrant must be specific about what can be searched and what can be seized during the search. To get a warrant, an officer must swear before a judge that he is acting according to the law.

After the First Amendment, the Fourth Amendment is probably the most well known to the average American. The founders wrote this amendment after having endured the tyranny of British soldiers conducting searches whenever they wanted, with no reasons given other than suspicion or to instill fear. Early American mistrust of government power came from the colonial experience itself. Most historians believe that the pivotal event was the Stamp Act, when taxes were imposed on every legal and business document, including newspapers, books, and pamphlets. Even more than the taxes themselves, the Americans resented the fact that a distant government in which they were not represented felt it had the right to regulate the printed opinions and ideas of the colonists. And they were further enraged by the ways in which the Stamp Act was enforced. Armed with "writs of assistance" issued by Parliament, British customs inspectors entered people's homes and ransacked their belongings in search of contraband even if they had no evidence of a Stamp

Colonists protest the Stamp Act in Boston. Enforcement of this policy included random searches of citizens' homes, a practice addressed by the Fourth Amendment. Today, a warrant would be required for such searches.

Act violation. The colonists came to hate these "warrantless" searches, and they became a rallying point for opposition to British rule.

Amendment V: Self-Incrimination and Due Process

The Fifth Amendment states that "No person shall be held to answer for a capital, or otherwise infamous crime, unless on a presentment or indictment of a Grand Jury, except in cases arising in the land or naval forces, or in the Militia, when in actual service in time of War or public danger; nor shall any person be subject for the same offence to be twice put in jeopardy of life or limb; nor shall be compelled in any criminal case to be a witness against himself, nor be deprived of life, liberty, or property, without due process of law; nor shall private property be taken for public use, without just compensation."

You have probably heard of people on trial or testifying before Congress "taking the Fifth." This refers to the Fifth Amendment, which gives American citizens the right to say nothing if what they say might be used to incriminate them. The Fifth Amendment prohibits punishment for a crime unless a person has been formally accused in writing. This discourages secret indictments and trials without the keeping of records, making it much harder for the government to arbitrarily punish people. This amendment also states that you cannot be put on trial a second time for the same crime. This is commonly called "double jeopardy." The government cannot keep prosecuting you over and over for a crime if you have once been judged innocent of that crime. In addition, the government can't take your property for public use unless they pay you a fair amount for it.

The Fifth Amendment was written to protect an accused person from abusive or corrupt practices by the government. The Founding Fathers wished to ensure that, while trials could be conducted and guilty criminals punished, innocent men and women wouldn't suffer by mere government whim. Sufficient evidence of criminal conduct has to be presented to a grand jury. The government cannot repeatedly try a person on the same charges until he or she is either convicted or acquitted. The government cannot demand answers from the accused, but instead must provide evidence of guilt, and it cannot take away property it wants or needs from its owner.

Amendment VI: Protecting the Accused

The Sixth Amendment states that "In all criminal prosecutions, the accused shall enjoy the right to a speedy and public trial, by an impartial jury of the State and district wherein the crime shall have been committed, which district shall have been previously ascertained by law, and to be informed of the nature and cause of the accusation; to be confronted with the witnesses against him; to have compulsory process for obtaining witnesses in his favor, and to have the Assistance of Counsel for his defense."

The Sixth Amendment protects those who are accused of crimes. The founders included this to prevent people from accusing others of crimes they did not commit simply out of jealousy or revenge, and to prevent the government from persecuting innocent citizens. According to the Sixth Amendment, a person accused of a crime cannot be held in jail waiting for his or her trial for an unreasonable amount of time. A trial is a public proceeding, not a secret one. Members of the jury must not be involved in the issue that is the subject of a trial. A trial must be in the court of the region in which the crime was committed. Suspects in a crime have to be told what they are accused of and the reason they are suspected. Finally, suspects get to hear and see the evidence against them, can present evidence in their defense, and can use a lawyer to help defend them against the charges.

Amendment VII: Federal Civil Cases

The Seventh Amendment states "In suits at common law, where the value in controversy shall exceed twenty dollars, the right of trial by jury shall be preserved, and no fact tried by a jury, shall be otherwise re-examined in any Court of the United States, than according to the rules of the common law."

The Seventh Amendment states that if you are being sued for more than twenty dollars, you can take the case to trial for a judgment. Whatever is decided in such a trial is final, unless another law says otherwise. The Seventh Amendment ensures that civil litigants are entitled to jury trials, just as the Sixth Amendment gives those accused of crimes the right to be tried by a jury of their peers. The amendment was written when it was noted near the end of the Constitutional Convention that no provision had yet been made for juries in civil cases. An attempt to add the provision was defeated, but the guarantee to the right of a jury in civil cases was one of the amendments urged on Congress by the ratifying conventions. The Seventh Amendment was finally passed without debate.

Amendment VIII: Cruel and Unusual Punishment

The Eighth Amendment states that "Excessive bail shall not be required, nor excessive fines imposed, nor cruel and unusual punishments inflicted." This amendment is commonly known as providing protection from cruel or unusual punishment. The Eighth Amendment protects those charged with crimes from punishment that is out of proportion to the crime committed. The intent of the amendment is to enforce the presumption of innocence until guilt has been proven, and to permit the accused the freedom to prepare an adequate defense. The Eighth Amendment comes from the English Bill of Rights of 1689.

Sometimes it may seem that judges set very high bail amounts. Bail may be deliberately increased, making it impossible for the defendant to pay. Bail is often calculated based on the danger the defendant may represent to the public if he or she is let out of jail. Court cases dealing with this issue have found that high bail amounts are not in violation of the Eighth Amendment.

Amendment IX: The Rights of the People

The Ninth Amendment states that "The enumeration in the Constitution, of certain rights, shall not be construed to deny or disparage others retained by the people." This means that simply listing these various rights does not imply that they are the only rights enjoyed by the citizens. The founders feared that, by listing rights not to be infringed by the government, rights that were not listed might be subject to government control because such control was not specifically prohibited. The Ninth Amendment was written to prevent such abuse.

The Ninth Amendment limits government powers solely to what was enumerated in the Constitution. If the founders forgot to mention some other right or protection commonly enjoyed by the people, the government could not assume that it regulated such unstated rights. For example, the specific right to privacy is not listed in the Bill of Rights, although it is strongly implied in the First, Third, Fourth, and Fifth Amendments. The right of American citizens to certain degrees of privacy has been protected in many court cases by the Ninth Amendment.

Amendment X: Authority of the States

The Tenth Amendment states "The powers not delegated to the United States by the Constitution, nor prohibited by it to the States, are reserved to the States respectively, or to the people." This means that the federal government cannot do anything the Constitution doesn't specifically say it can do. When the Bill of Rights was being considered, the states didn't want to lose the right to make regional decisions, nor did they want to be subject to an overriding power from a distant national capital.

The Tenth Amendment was written to ensure the states that they would remain largely in charge of activities within their own borders. The states can do anything they want as long as the action or law isn't within the constitutional power of the federal government, or prohibited by the Constitution. Essentially, the Tenth Amendment says that if there is no law against something, then it is legal until the courts decide otherwise.

Rights, But Not for All

The Bill of Rights was written in a broad language that excluded no one, but it was not intended to protect all Americans. At the time, women were considered the property of their husbands, so the

Bill of Rights was rarely thought to pertain to them. Women were unable to vote until 1920, when the Nineteenth Amendment was passed and ratified. An attempt to pass an Equal Rights Amendment in 1972 fell three states short of ratification.

The Bill of Rights was in force for nearly 135 years before Congress granted Native Americans the same rights as American citizens. Native Americans

The Nineteenth Amendment guaranteed women the right to vote. Here, a room full of women witness Missouri Governor Frederick Gardner signing ratification of the Nineteenth Amendment on January 6, 1920.

were considered aliens, despite the fact that they inhabited the land of the United States long before European settlers arrived. They were governed not by ordinary American laws, but by federal treaties and statutes that removed from tribes most of their land and autonomy.

Slavery was in full force in the United States when the Bill of Rights was written. Even the founders of the new nation owned slaves. So there was an implicit understanding that there was a race

Since many of the Founding Fathers owned slaves, it is no surprise that the Bill of Rights did not consider African Americans when it was guaranteeing rights to the individual. In fact, the Constitution was used to protect slavery.

exception to the Constitution. For the first seventy-eight years after it was ratified, the Constitution protected slavery and legalized racial suppression and separation. Instead of constitutional rights, slaves were governed by slave codes that controlled every part of their lives. They could not go to court, make contracts, or own property. They could be whipped, branded, imprisoned without trial, and hanged. It would take years of struggle and a bloody civil war before additional amendments to the Constitution were passed, giving slaves and their descendants the full rights of citizenship. The Thirteenth Amendment, passed in 1865, abolished slavery. The Fourteenth Amendment guaranteed to African Americans the rights of due process and equal protection of the law, and the Fifteenth Amendment gave them the right to vote. But it would be nearly another century before these rights were enforced.

Appendix
The Bill of Rights

The Preamble to The Bill of Rights

Congress of the United States

begun and held at the City of New-York, on

Wednesday the fourth of March, one thousand seven hundred and eighty nine.

THE Conventions of a number of the States, having at the time of their adopting the Constitution, expressed a desire, in order to prevent misconstruction or abuse of its powers, that further declaratory and restrictive clauses should be added: And as extending the ground of public confidence in the Government, will best ensure the beneficent ends of its institution.

RESOLVED by the Senate and House of Representatives of the United States of America, in Congress assembled, two thirds of both Houses concurring, that the following Articles be proposed to the Legislatures of the several States, as amendments to the Constitution of the United

States, all, or any of which Articles, when ratified by three fourths of the said Legislatures, to be valid to all intents and purposes, as part of the said Constitution; viz.

ARTICLES in addition to, and Amendment of the Constitution of the United States of America, proposed by Congress, and ratified by the Legislatures of the several States, pursuant to the fifth Article of the original Constitution.

Amendment I

Congress shall make no law respecting an establishment of religion, or prohibiting the free exercise thereof; or abridging the freedom of speech, or of the press; or the right of the people peaceably to assemble, and to petition the Government for a redress of grievances.

Amendment II

A well regulated Militia, being necessary to the security of a free State, the right of the people to keep and bear Arms, shall not be infringed.

Amendment III

No Soldier shall, in time of peace be quartered in any house, without the consent of the Owner, nor in time of war, but in a manner to be prescribed by law.

Amendment IV

The right of the people to be secure in their persons, houses, papers, and effects, against unreasonable searches and seizures, shall not be violated, and no Warrants shall issue, but upon probable cause, supported by Oath or affirmation, and particularly describing the place to be searched, and the persons or things to be seized.

Amendment V

No person shall be held to answer for a capital, or otherwise infamous crime, unless on a presentment or indictment of a Grand Jury, except in cases arising in the land or naval forces, or in the Militia, when in actual service in time of War or public danger; nor shall any person be subject for the same offence to be twice put in jeopardy of life or limb; nor shall be compelled in any criminal case to be a witness against himself, nor be deprived of life, liberty, or property, without due process of law; nor shall private property be taken for public use, without just compensation.

Amendment VI

In all criminal prosecutions, the accused shall enjoy the right to a speedy and public trial, by an impartial jury of the State and district wherein the crime shall have been committed, which district shall have been previously ascertained by law, and to be informed of the nature and cause of the accusation; to be confronted with the witnesses against him; to have compulsory process for obtaining witnesses in his favor, and to have the Assistance of Counsel for his defence.

Amendment VII

In Suits at common law, where the value in controversy shall exceed twenty dollars, the right of trial by jury shall be preserved, and no fact tried by a jury, shall be otherwise re-examined in any Court of the United States, than according to the rules of the common law.

Amendment VIII

Excessive bail shall not be required, nor excessive fines imposed, nor cruel and unusual punishments inflicted.

Amendment IX

The enumeration in the Constitution, of certain rights, shall not be construed to deny or disparage others retained by the people.

Amendment X

The powers not delegated to the United States by the Constitution, nor prohibited by it to the States, are reserved to the States respectively, or to the people.

Glossary

amendment—Any change proposed or made to a bill or motion by adding to, substituting, or omitting from the existing document.

Articles of Confederation—The governing agreement first made by the original thirteen states of the United States. They were adopted March 1, 1781, and remained the law until March 1789.

delegate—A person authorized to act as a representative for others.

levy—To impose or collect a tax.

Loyalist—A colonist during the American Revolution who favored the British side. Also called a Tory.

monopoly—Exclusive control by one group producing or selling a commodity or service.

Parliament—The national legislature of the United Kingdom, made up of the House of Lords and the House of Commons.

preamble—An introduction or opening paragraph of a document, usually stating the overall purpose of the document.

ratify—To sign an agreement or document into validation.

redcoats—British soldiers in the Revolutionary era, who wore red uniforms.

repeal—To revoke by an official or formal act.

sovereignty—Complete independence and self-government.

tyranny—A government in which a single ruler has absolute power.

Further Reading

Amar, Akhil Reed and Les Adams. *The Bill of Rights Primer*. New York: Skyhorse Publishing, 2013.

Beeman, Richard. *Plain, Honest Men: The American Constitution*. New York: Random House, 2010.

Krensky, Stephen. *The Bill of Rights*. New York: Marshal Cavendish Benchmark, 2012.

Madison, James. *The Constitutional Convention: A Narrative History From the Notes of James Madison*. New York: Modern Library, 2005.

Maier, Pauline. *Ratification: The People Debate the Constitution, 1787–1788*. New York: Simon & Schuster, 2011.

Pederson, Charles E. *The U.S. Constitution & Bill of Rights*. Edina, Minn.: Abdo Publishing Company, 2010.

Web Sites

aclu.org

The American Civil Liberties Union (ACLU) defends and preserves the individual rights and liberties that the Constitution and laws of the United States guarantee everyone in the country.

billofrightsinstitute.org

The Bill of Rights Institute educates young people about the words and ideas of America's Founders, the liberties guaranteed in our Founding documents, and how our Founding principles continue to affect and shape a free society.

archives.gov

The National Archives and Records Administration preserves and documents government and historical records and makes them available to the public at the National Archives.

Bibliography

Archiving Early America. Retrieved April 2002 (http://www.earlyamerica.com/index.html).

Bowen, Catherine Drinker. *Miracle at Philadelphia: The Story of the Constitutional Convention, May to September 1787.* Vol. 1. Boston: Little, Brown & Company, 1986.

Clancy, Christopher H. *Constitutional Litigation.* New York: Practicing Law Institute, 1971.

Coleman, Warren. *The Bill of Rights.* Chicago: Children's Press, 1987.

The Constitution Society. Retrieved May 2002 (http://www.constitution.org).

Encyclopaedia Brittanica Online. Retrieved May 2002 (http://www.britannica.com).

Know Your Rights! Retrieved May 2002 (http://www.harbor-net.com/rights/states.html).

Lady Liberty's Constitution Clearing House. Retrieved April 2002 (http://www.ladylibrty.com/bill_of_rights.html).

Livingston, William S. *Federalism and Constitutional Change.* Westport, Conn.: Greenwood Press, 1974.

The National Archives and Records Administration. Retrieved April 2002 (http://www.archives.gov/exhibit_hall/charters_of_freedom/bill_of_rights/bill_of_rights.html).

The United States Constitution Online. Retrieved April 2002 (http://www.usconstitution.net/index.html).

Index